MAXIMS

OF A

MAGICIAN

I0087436

RICHY ROY

PRESTIGE BOOK PUBLISHING

THIS IS A GOURAMI BOOK
BY PRESTIGE BOOK PUBLISHING

Copyright © 2019 by Richard Roy
All rights reserved. Published in Canada by
Prestige Book Publishing

Paperback ISBN: 978-1-9990971-0-3
eBook ISBN: 978-1-9990971-1-0
Printed by KDP
Published May 01, 2019
First Edition

Praise for Maxims of a Magician

"Finally, a book for magicians that offers performance experience. Save yourself ten years of trial and error and read this book instead! Richy Roy has the ability to say what no other magic book does. His insight and knowledge on business in magic and performance tips will elevate and improve your show today. I wish someone had told me these tips back when I started magic because this is a lot of years experience found in this one book. Well worth the read, thank you Richy."

- Matt Gore (International Award-Winning Magician)

"This book is chock full of important tips on what it takes to be a performing magician and should be right next to 'Strong Magic' and all of the other books that teach real magic and not just tricks."

- Shaun Robison, The Charming Deceptionist

"The maxims in this book are a game changer. It helped me take my show to another level of professionalism. It helped me change some of my average magic tricks into creating that magical moment the audience wants. My show, my business, and my character have seen sudden improvements from implementing these maxims into my daily routines."

- Doug Dern (Mentalist/Magician)

"Overall, the book is informative and lays out exactly what is needed to be a successful magician.

Lots of us magicians have learned these lessons through trial and error. I think magicians of all levels will benefit greatly from many of these maxims."

-    Jamie O'Brien (Magic by Jamie)

"Richy Roy has done something I hope the magic community at large will embrace. He has not only shown the path to elevating magic to its rightful place as a true art form next to dance, theater, music and painting, he has also given the rungs of the ladder to get there. For those seeking a book of tricks or sleight of hand routines, you may want to come back to this later. For those interested in a professional career in magic or mentalism, than this book is for you! Easy to read in small powerful statements, "Maxims of a Magician" is sure to become a classic. I hope others will feel the same that this stands with The Books of Wonder, The Fitzkee Trilogy and The Tarbell Course in Magic as one of the great contributions to our beloved art!"

-    Michael Finazzo (Underground Mentalist)

Introduction

To a magician of the distant past, having access to a wealth of knowledge at our fingertips would seem like a fantasy. Today, that dream is a reality. In an instant we can peruse e-zines, download video tutorials, study eBooks, dig through forums, participate in group discussions, connect with peers and mentors, sign up for online classes, and even take part in a distant conference right from the comfort of our office chair.

But with all the benefits our connectivity brings, the Internet also brings with it perilous downfalls for both the creators and consumers. The wide-spread plague of misinformation, wildly uneducated biased opinions, unauthorized dissemination of other's intellectual property, and the endless enigma of white-noise to name only a few. The merits and deficiencies of the internet can be argued at great lengths, but the point of interest, pertaining to this work is that of the young magician who rarely considers the valuable lessons that can only be learned from the experience of performing magic for an audience and the insight that can be gathered by having face to face conversations with professional magicians and their peers. All mentors know that a conversation over a shared bottle is much different than a Skype meeting where each remains in the confines of their residence. It is during these cherished moments of life that we learn true lessons that aid us in our successful magic careers. Conversely, technology seems to act as a membrane that filters out that special unperceivable quality that true social engagements bring us.

Some of this information can be found deep within the classic books of magic, various magic magazines, and in interviews with today's successful magicians. The problem here is that it would literally take thousands of hours to read and listen for these golden nuggets of knowledge. And if you are like eighty percent of the people in this world, chances are that you do not enjoy reading in the first place. And even if you do enjoy reading, chances are slim that you will read through an entire text of eighty-five-thousand words and retain all the information. Or with the wide range of lectures and podcasts available, consider the challenge of deciding which one to listen to and maintaining the attention span to listen to the thousands of hours uploaded to the net. Indeed, this appears to be a great challenge, especially if you are an amateur magician who does not know where to start.

The value of this book is that many of these unwritten laws of magic have been distilled into maxims that are easy to remember. Through years of study, observations, discussions, and experience as a professional magician, I have recorded what I consider to be some of the most important lessons that contribute to the success of a magician. As previously stated, some of these lessons can be found in current magic literature or draw comparisons to everyday life philosophies, but many of these lessons have not been published, put into context from a magician's point of view, or simply compiled into one concise document. The lessons have also been compressed to make for easy reading, in the hopes that any magician whom picks up this edition will be able to read through to the end without falling victim to boredom or time constraints.

This book is not meant to be read once and left to be forgotten about on the shelf. This book should be frequently revisited and serve as a guide to help maintain focus throughout one's journey in the world of entertainment.

If I could go back in time to when I was a young and ambitious magician, this would be the one book I wish I could have read at the beginning. Now, as an older, experienced, professional magician, I have referred back to these notes again and again, and they have always guided me in making the correct decision. I fear that the magicians who could benefit the most from this book will never even give it a consideration.

Perhaps I should follow my own advice and turn this into an instant downloadable video MasterClass and include my devilishly clever method and version of Colour Match... but that sounds like another project for another time.

Foreword

As you read these pages of wisdom, your mind may drift off and imagine circumstances you've faced before. Many of these thoughts are relatable.

You may also drift off into thought because you have never considered the philosophy or thoughts expressed.

You may discover a few new thoughts and put them where you can refer to them before stepping on a stage.

You may not have a stage except for the ability to perform strolling magic. These thoughts and ideas are about structure and appearance so an actual stage is not necessarily needed.

You may be in the middle of a routine when something you read here causes you to become more engaged or gives you more focus so the experience is relevant to the audience at hand.

What you are about to learn may seem akin to reading the thoughts of Confucius, for magicians. Any way you look at it, these writings are relevant through the ages and 100 years from now may be used as lessons that never go out of style.

Jay Leslie

Preface

This book is for all magicians: amateurs and professionals, workers and hobbyists, part-timers and full-timers, young and old, and everyone in-between.

Recently an IBM Ring was brought back to life in my local area and with the introductions to some new faces in the magic community, I started asking myself "What would I want to know if I was entering the world of magic?" and also "What *should* I know as I enter the world of magic?" The latter question being of higher importance.

There are many things in the world of entertainment that you will only learn through experience or by overhearing a discussion amongst veteran magicians. There are also many intangible qualities a magician develops from logging hundreds of hours in front of an audience. But the truth is many magicians do not take the time to reflect on the things that have made them successful; therefore, it never gets discussed or published for others to learn. It is something we just come to know after performing for a few decades.

These things become unspoken truths. Successful magicians know them and growing magicians should know them, but the former rarely teach them and the latter never know to ask because they don't know they even exist.

A brief list of resources available to magicians on the market teach things such as magic skills, techniques, and methods, theory on performance and dramatic structure, lessons about scripting and developing routines, or how to use psychology or comedy to an entertainer's benefit. But rarely discussed are the valuable philosophies, general truths, and rules of conduct that are known to experienced magicians.

This book was written for all magicians to benefit. I encourage you to read through these pages with your local Ring of magicians and discuss each point together, openly as a group. Through open discourse we uncover different points of views that we cannot see on our own and in the end, everyone benefits to a greater extent.

To the inexperienced magicians, I hope it serves as an important resource to stimulate your growth. To the experienced magicians, I hope it serves as a reminder of our virtues and vices.

On a personal note, I do hope that I have created here a valuable contribution to our magic community, something with a little more depth than simply a different method to perform ACAAN. If I am able to change just one magician's career for the better, then I will be content.

Is this a complete collection of wisdom in the field of magic? Far from it, but it is a good start and we all need a starting point. So what better place then right here, right now.

Sincerely;

Richy Roy

1

Intelligence and Charisma

These are the two components of a masterful magician; if you lack one and have strength in the other, you are simply incomplete. Having a shining personality is not enough; knowledge of performance, magic theory, skill, and the like are also needed.

2

Make Your Own Choices

The naïve magicians will fail to succeed when they do not choose for themselves but let fate and luck be the master of their decisions. Take control of your career, roster of clients, status, and circle of friends and colleagues of your choice.

3

Conceal Your Projects
in the Works

When people are teased with the unknown, it heightens the importance of your success. It is dangerous to show everything, all the time. Hold your cards close to your chest. If you do not let on to your workings immediately, it builds excitement and elevates expectation. Adding mystery to your life's work is expected from lay people and fellow magicians alike. When you finally explain, do not be overly detailed. This should be similar to casual conversations you have on a daily basis where you do not express your innermost and deepest thoughts and feelings. Being carefully quiet is wise advice from elder entertainers. When you state your intentions and ambitions in great detail, it only draws out trolls and critics. And if you do not meet people's expectations, you will experience twice the pain in your failure.

4

Wisdom and Bravery

These are pieces of our greatest magicians. It takes much courage and knowledge to be more than an average entertainer. Never stop challenging to become braver and never stop learning to become wise. But each of these elements needs to work together. Wisdom lets us see what needs to be done and how to do it. Our strength and courage allows us to accomplish what needs to be done. It is of no use to have the ability to perform but lack the courage to stand in front of an audience. Likewise, it would be a mistake to command attention on center stage without understanding how a magician creates a magician experience. A magician without knowledge is like a stage without lights.

5

Have Others Depend On You

The smart magician knows it is better to have clients needing him than thanking him. To keep your clients hoping you will come and perform again is far better than clients thanking you for coming. Hope is a great memory; gratitude is a bad memory. You will have more work from dependency than from courtesy. Once a client has had their fill, they will cast you aside. Many know to leave their audience wanting more; many forget to leave their client wanting more as well. Keep their hope alive by delivering strong but never entirely satisfying in order to make yourself always needed. But don't overdo it, or it will be the death of your relationship. Always leave them wanting more.

6

A Magician Continually Grows

We are not born magicians. Each day we grow and become better entertainers until we reach the ultimate status of master magician, one who is full of accomplishments and greatness. We know these master magicians by their taste in magic, the conviction of their clear thoughts, their ability to make the right decisions, and their high level of self-mastery. Most magicians never become masters or feel complete because something is always missing or lacking and few magicians hit their peak late in life. But even a master magician continues to grow and learn, for the art of magic is forever growing and filled with mysteries.

7

Do Not Upstage Your Headliner

Outshining your superiors creates hatred and can be fatal to your career as a growing magician. In their minds, they are the celebrities and wish to be regarded as such. They will let you help them, but they won't let you pass them. Be careful with advice you give, even if it comes with best intentions. Make it look like it is something they may have forgotten about rather than something they never knew. Envy, ill will, and egotism run ramped amongst magicians and never leave, no matter how successful they become.

8

Self-control is Freedom to Perform

This is one of the highest qualities an entertainer can have. A magician's career will be filled with adversity and mastering yourself is the key to overcome those obstacles. When your temptations take over, do not let it destroy your reputation, especially if you are high on the ladder. Having complete control over your desires is the best way to avoid trouble and protect yourself. The road offers plenty of temptations for the traveling entertainer; do not fall into the trap that has destroyed many.

9

Avoid the Faults of the Magic Community

A magician is always part of the community regardless of their proclamations. Some successful magicians, more than others, will always be more involved with the magic community and will owe much of their success to those around them. It takes cleverness to overcome the negative perceptions clients and lay people may have about magicians. You will gain extra credit for not being like the others because people don't expect it, which is highly appreciated and often sought after. Erase the stereotypes that plague magicians by proving them wrong through example.

10

Fortune and Fame

Money comes and money goes, but fame is forever. Money will be for this life and fame will be for after. Fortune can be gained quickly, but fame is earned throughout a career. The want of fame comes from good intentions but is earned from extremes; either brilliant masters of our art or horrible wrecks of giant proportions. The true prize is to have one's name written in the history books, but be forewarned that this comes with a price most are unwilling to pay.

11

Build Relationships With Magicians Who Can Teach You

Allow your friendship to be your master-class and learn the culture of successful magicians through conversations. Your friends will become your teachers as you mix the pleasure of discussion with the benefit of education. Conversations will involve being rewarded with acknowledgment from what you say and gaining knowledge through listening. The student will understand that listening is the key just as talking too much is the unopened padlock to the wealth of wisdom.

12

Magic and Materials

Magic props do not make the magician just as shoes do not make the basketball player. Focus on adding art to magic routines to fix the bad and improve the good of all routines. A magical device or illusion rarely gives us what is best; for that, we must turn to art. No matter how good a purchased item may be, it will always remain lacking and uncultured if the magician is not trained up from the grounds of art. We all struggle with some aspect that is untrained, and we all have strengths that need polishing.

13

Attention to Circumstance

The magical effect itself is not enough; the way it is done is also needed. A sloppy presentation wrecks every effect—even the best of tricks. A relatable meaning enhances everything and makes old effects beautiful once again. Presented with good intentions is the way to a person's heart. The refined routine is the joy of the presentation and a pleasant presence will help any difficult situation.

14

Be Accessible to Magical Thinkers

The strong magicians surround themselves with the champions of magic and distance themselves from the trolls who only live to create difficulties. It is of even more importance to know how to make use of the knowledgeable. It is an impressive skill, and the fastest path to success, to have our superior magicians in our corner working with us to reach our heights. Open your social floodgates to those who have broken road before you. Studying without effort is the daily path one must travel. And then, when you speak to many other magicians, you are speaking from the many great magicians that you studied with, improving your status with little effort. The greatest books on magic were written from knowledge distilled from many great minds. If you cannot have these great magicians working for you, have them as your friends and keep them close.

15

Mean Well and Stay Keen

Master magicians know that both are important in order to have continued success in entertainment. To be smart but have bad intentions is to create a bomb waiting to explode. If you have bad intentions from the start, it will damage all other perfections. If paired with great intellect, it makes it that much more pronounced.

16

Apply Yourself and Be Skillful

Most average magicians will never succeed because they lack one or the other. Success comes to the magicians that train to be skilled and constantly work and perform. Average magicians will gain more by doing than skilled magicians will by not doing. To gain your reputation, you must work for it. Just like trinkets, things that cost little have very little worth. In some cases, the magician that constantly goes out and performs, and performs often, will land better contracts than magicians that live downstairs with supreme talent. Once you craft your act with skill and art, apply yourself before an audience. Be a doer. Just as the old saying goes "Knowledge is power, but knowledge without action is useless."

17

Be Modest With Your Beginnings

Do not build up exaggerated expectations when you begin a new project. It is a great failure to not fulfill your fan's hopes, for this is the surest way to lose them. What we bring to the stage cannot equal the imagined because it is easy for people to create unbound expectations, but it is hard for entertainers to deliver. However excellent your new act, which you've promised and promoted, is, it will never meet the audience'sexpectations if overblown and exaggerated. And when your audience finds themselves disappointed with their expectations, you will not find them returning to future performances. Instead, the great magician knows to build curiosity slowly without committing himself to a final outcome. It is better to exhibit a much greater performance and have people leaving the auditorium believing your show was better than what was thought prior.

18

Be a Magician of Modern Times

Make use of the time we live in to deliver a modern version of magic. Some magical routines and illusions have had their time—it is best to leave them there. Even the most excellent acts have had their time when they were in fashion. Magic theory and wisdom is the one exception that surpasses all because it remains timeless.

19

Learn To Be Lucky

There are rules to luck that great entertainers do not leave to chance. Luck can be helped with care and attention. Place yourself in front of opportunity, waiting for it to shine on you. Bold magicians do better than the average by constantly pushing forward. Persistence is lady luck's boyfriend. But the master magicians know, above all, that there truly is no good or bad luck aside from being wise or being foolish. Luck is when hard work meets opportunity.

20

Learn To Live With Misery

The magician that turns pro has committed himself to live through hell, whether he knows it or not. He will experience humiliation, rejection, self-doubt, ridicule, isolation, and worthlessness. Great magicians have learned to love living miserably and can wear it as a badge of honour. Living with mental hardships is an ingredient most will think is unique to them but is universal to artists alike. Remember this the next time you choose to engage a critical conversation with your fellow magician because you never know the exact struggles they are fighting, but you can be sure there are many.

21

Control Your Imagination

Sometimes you must reel it in, sometimes give it a push. Its importance keeps our happiness in check and keeps you reasonable. A wild imagination will pollute your mind with visions of grandeur and will keep you feeling discontent. To others, the imagination will promise excitement and adventure with happy delusions. The young magician will rush out with only delusions to bolster their aspirations. Whereas the seasoned entertainer knows to take his time and uses self-control, the key to keeping his imagination in check.

22

Know How to Read Into
Conversations

Colleagues rarely like to state your faults, but the ones with good intentions will drop you hints. Unfortunately, this no longer seems to be good enough. We have to know how to take a hint from those lending us advice. People will not understand you if you cannot understand others. When a great magician takes time to help you out, they will only speak half-truths, but if we pay close attention then we can understand what they are truly trying to say. As a new magician growing and learning, we tend to wear ears that only hear praise. The successful magicians wear ears that catch criticisms. Look for these nuggets of advice to climb higher.

23

Excellence Lives in Quality

Ten superior magic routines will outshine a hundred mediocre acts. The best ones are always rare; having too many routines simply lowers value. The master magician has a pocket of utilities that can outshine a trailer full of props. Learn to tame the allure of many gaffs and gimmicks and learn to understand the value of a standard deck. Focus on mastering your ambitious card before learning the entire card college.

24

Refuse to Be Common

Deliberately put in work at expanding your taste. The great magicians learned early on to stray from the most popular tricks that pleased the masses. The true critics of performance art are rarely satisfied with acts that elicit common applause. By the time you gravitate and educate yourself in popular fads, they will have already come to pass by the time you take the stage. And when you finally do perform your work, it becomes muddled with the rest of the magicians performing the exact same thing.

25

Avoid the Unlucky

Bad luck is usually found amongst the fools, and unfortunately, there is nothing more contagious. Be cautious that you do not associate with hack magicians and corrupt agents/clients, as more will inevitably find their way into your career. Instead, follow the process of successful magicians; sooner or later the lucky magician always wins the great contracts.

26

Develop a Reputation For Helping Out Other Magicians.

Universally, being gracious is looked upon as being the highest of goodwill. What you put in to your community of magicians, you will get out tenfold. That is the biggest advantage of having the status of being a great magician— having the ability to help up-and-coming magicians. By helping others, your network will grow and you will benefit along the way.

27

Know How to Pull Away

It's important to learn how to remove yourself from a bad client relationship or disastrous production. There are many colleagues and clients who know how to eat away at your valuable time. To be tied up with these people and matters that don't concern you is worse than not doing anything. It is not enough to see that these people don't bother us and waste our time; we also must be careful not to waste other's time as well. With colleagues and magic friends, we shouldn't abuse their help or demand more from them then they are able or willing to give. Use moderation when reaching out to others. Overextending your reach can do more damage than one ever expects.

28

Know Your Greatest Quality

Understand your strongest gift and cultivate it to assist the rest. Every magician has a unique quality they can excel in; they just need to realize it. When you notice which quality puts you ahead of other magicians, take charge of it and use it to your advantage. In the world of magic, it is far too easy to be distracted and swayed towards developing a weakness that will not help you succeed. Ask your mentor which quality they should have focused on in their early career and you will notice that all have a different opinion because all have different natural strengths and gifts. Find your greatest quality soon to succeed faster.

29

Think Over Your Act

The unprepared magician looks just as foolish as the magician who has not thought about the routine he presents. They never bother to ask "Why am I doing this?" or "What is my motivation for doing that?" and it ends up being insincere and less effective. Many magicians never learn to think of why they're performing an effect. This important step should be of the utmost importance and always kept in mind. Always consider that there is more to your magic routines than what you are currently thinking. This way, your comprehension of why you are performing it will grow and lead to a fuller act. Step back and give your act a final look through the eyes of the audience, for they will perceive it differently than we have grown accustomed to. Ensure it is simple to follow, for as Ortiz points out "Audiences are easily confused but not easily fooled."

30

Keep a File of Prepared Lines and Know When to Use Them

This is the secret of great magicians looking naturally funny or engaging on stage. These lines are often used in specific moments throughout the performance to test the crowd's mood and responsiveness. By using these phrases selectively and judiciously, we can penetrate the audience's guard and begin to make a connection. If these lines should look off the cuff and improvised then it will work in your favour, confirming your status as a seasoned entertainer and will enhance your reputation. The key to accessing this file of prepared lines is to be completely comfortable and in total control of your performance, any distraction will inhibit your quick wit. But beware of age old canned lines; some were funny the first time they were heard, most were never funny to begin with.

31

Recognize When a Routine is at its Peak and Know When to Use it

With proper attention, magic routines will reach a point of excellence. Up until then, they keep improving, until after time they become dated and less relevant. Few routines reach the point that they cannot be improved upon. A great magician recognizes when the routine is hottest and knows to enjoy performing it. Only the truly artful routines remain timeless; study these and know them well.

32

Never Finish With Your Strongest Effect

Like any great novel, the most thrilling or dramatic part happens near the end, but never on the last page. The structure of your act should leave the audience wanting more, but they should also feel satisfied as if they've eaten a five-course meal. The final act of our show is for inviting the audience to become emotionally attached to us, make inferences, or to have them consider our point of view by making connections in their own lives. It is in our nature to expect conclusions to the stories we invest in. The strongest effect is the turning point, not the epilogue.

33

Give Permission for Applause

An audience is apprehensive by nature. When they enter our arena, they will not engage in playing the game until they understand the rules. It is our job to free their apprehensions and promote engagement. If not, then few will reach out on their own accord and most will remain reserved in fear of looking foolish or disruptive. But be careful not to continually dictate cues. An audience will quickly grow tiresome and can turn if they feel pressed to perform for us.

34

Always Warm Up Your Audience

Just as chef would never throw a porterhouse steak onto a cold barbeque, a seasoned entertainer will never further the act until raising the crowd's temperature. Live entertainment has never been a one-way street. No, it is built on reciprocity and engagement. It is much easier to open the doors first before entering their hearts and minds instead of forcing your way through with a battering ram of rehearsed patter and dazzle.

35

Finish Your Performance While the Crowd is Still on Your Side

All the best magicians do it. A beautiful exit is just as effective as an explosive entrance. A too long performance becomes tiresome and unwelcomed, but ending before they've had their fill leaves hope for your next performance. The longer your performance, the greater risk of losing lustre. The most memorable performances have been made from the intensity of strong magic displayed in short durations.

36

Natural On-Stage Presence

It is the secret sauce of master magicians that do not lean heavily on magic itself. Audiences respond to it without knowing why, recognizing the entertainment value of a magician with charisma and confidence. These magicians are entertainers by excellence and have success through privilege.

37

Control Your Hostilities Towards Other Magicians

We often and easily start disliking other magicians, especially within our circles, before we even know anything about them. Sometimes this natural hatred even gets attached to master magicians. But it quickly becomes clear that there is nothing worse to our reputation than disliking magicians better than us. Disliking them only eats away at our character and brings us down.

38

Become a Magician With Great Depth

Your inner being must be at least as impressive as your exterior. Some magicians' characters are only developed for the stage and are a farce in social situations. Clients do not want to be bored by your drivel when negotiating business matters, and they can be swift to pick up on who you truly are immediately after introductions. Keep your words flowing smooth and your ears receptive to answer their needs. People will easily trust entertainers they enjoy conversing with. It is a key ingredient of unlocking coveted performance contracts.

39

Do Not Lose Your Self-Respect and Don't Become Too Self-Conscious

Allow your integrity to guide you to what is right and keep your morals stricter than your best client would expect of you. Keep your reputation clean more for your own self-respect but also for the client's eye. A fragile self-worth is an invitation for resentment and the match that burns bridges.

40

Choose Your Material Well

Your career depends on this. You need great taste and exceedingly good judgement. The difficulty lies in the fact that neither intellect nor research will help in this area. To choose well, you require two things: to be able to make a decision at all, and the discernment to choose best. There are many brilliant magicians that have great judgement, are very knowledgeable, and have keen observations but still have difficulty making decisions. Learning how to choose well will save time, money, pain, and regrets.

41

Ensure Your Routines Mean Something to You

It's simply not good enough to create magic that has meaning. If it doesn't concern yourself, the audience shall pick up on it and see you as insincere. And if you cannot fool them with your patter, your insincerity will surely detract from the magic moments.

42

If You Are Not Funny, Don't Try to Be

An entertainer that cannot deliver comedy, but tries, is like watching a baby giraffe learning to walk for the first time. It is awkward and comical for all the wrong reasons. Never create a reason for your audience to turn against you. We are here to create magic. Creating laughs is secondary to our true purpose; therefore, magic can be done very well without comedy.

43

Master Your Openings

No one in the crowd truly believes that you care how they are doing tonight, so don't ask them. It is our job as magicians to improve their emotional state regardless of how they are currently feeling. Do away with informal pleasantries one might have in conversations. You are here to entertain, so be entertaining! We only have one chance to make a first impression; the rest of the performance will be judged on that so make it worthy. Command their immediate attention and leave them no room to question whether or not you deserve their admiration. Strike quickly and steal their hearts the moment you hit the stage. Any delays will detract from the entire performance.

44

Never Be Upset or Make a Scene in the Public Eye.

Any outburst is only perceived as a great embarrassment. If you redline at a moment's notice, you may kill your career such as Michael Richards did in a small comedy club. Therefore, it is vitally important to be in control of our emotions at all times. Even in the worst circumstances we cannot let go of our self-control and risk damaging our reputation, but rather enhance it by showing mastery of our emotions.

45

Respect Your Audience's Intelligence

Do not be tedious with your patter, telling them what you're doing every step of the way. If it doesn't bore them to death, it will surely confuse them when you inevitably ramble. Simply telling them a falsehood to cover a move is too elementary to strengthen any routine. Magicians are to be compared to other entertainers that adore their audience, not to be compared with politicians and lawyers that love people's wallets. Employ 'Chekhov's Gun' and be economical with your words, this is a sign of a masterful magician.

46

Always Thank the Sponsors

Understand where your paycheque is coming from and what is expected of you. Make your client look good by taking the initiative to acknowledge their benefactors. An overlooked expectation can be the deal breaker on future engagements, so the wise magician ensures his script is created with this in mind. Your performance today is your audition for tomorrow's performance; be sure to take advantage of every opportunity.

47

Be Persistent and Intelligent

Persistence executes what intelligence carefully planned. Rushing to do something before proper examination is where amateur magicians will fail. They do not know the potential obstacles or the amount of work required for most endeavours. The intelligent magicians who procrastinate will fail more often. Do your work immediately and your riches will be on the horizon. Begin your work early and leave nothing for tomorrow. He who wins the morning wins the day.

48

Learn to Slow Down

A studied magician appears to have complete control of his performance when he is not rushing. First control yourself before you can control the audience. Pacing controls more suspense and mystery and garners a greater applause than simply skipping to the sudden revelation. We must also know how to wait when developing skill sets. The foolish magician takes to the stage with an unsteady hand. Mastering any such manipulation requires persistence of practice and tenacity. The greatest challenge is identifying when you are finally ready to take stage and not a moment sooner.

49

Appear Professional at All Times

Someone is watching at any given moment. Every action is noted and reflects your level of professionalism. A true professional dresses, speaks, moves, and acts the same even when others are not present. Integrity is the blood of your manners; lose too much and one will surely fall in status.

50

Adapt Yourself to Your Crowd

There is no need to demonstrate all your abilities to every type of audience. Exhibit no more delights than necessary. If your repertoire is displayed in full, there will be nothing to show tomorrow. Always keep an extra trick up your sleeve. Presenting fresh material each day wins a larger subscription and hides the limits of your capacity. Become a magician of unlimited magic in their imaginations.

51

Prepare a Brilliant Finale

People take away two things from a great performance: the best moments and the worst faults. Never should the crowd leave the auditorium with a sour taste in their mouths from boredom or bearing witness to meaningless drivel. The great magician understands to think of the finale first, and attach more importance to a positive exit than to grand applause on entrance. It is far too common to witness inexperienced magicians that have spectacular beginnings and very dull endings. The main point is that most will already be granted a warm welcome anyway; therefore, focus on the overall feeling upon completion. Master magicians earn a standing ovation and are felt to deserve an encore from strategically building the structure of their routings and ending brilliantly.

52

Shine Bright in What is Excellent

It is rare to see a magician master the most difficult of illusions. You cannot become a great magician without excelling in something that outshines the rest. Average never garners roaring applause. The master of a difficult and brilliant manipulation will live amongst the exceptional and separate themselves from the plethora of simple, single production performers.

53

Leave the Enjoyment for Your Audience

The professional has worked hard to develop strong material; there is no need to laugh at his own jokes, just like there is no need to be amazed at his own miracles. Coaxing a crowd only cheapens a great performance and signals insecurities.

54

Keep a Collection of 'Outs' at Your Disposal

Know that it is important to stay practiced on methods of recovering from disaster. Think about and consider ways to salvage a routine so as to be ready at a moment's notice, and then rehearse until mastered. It does no good to keep it only in one's mind for it will never be thought of when needed most. Bring your strategies into your hands on your own time so that you will be prepared when the unexpected inevitably takes place.

55

Do Not Perform Filler

Each routine has a purpose that works to enhance the completeness of your show. Anything less shall detract. It is our duty as entertainers to fulfill the agreed upon contract with our audience. They give us their time and we reward them with delights. With only a short window to display our life's work, we should not waste the occasion with inferior material or we risk being judged solely on that portion.

56

Respect Your Restraints

If you have been given a set amount of time to perform, be thankful for every minute and do not step over a second more. Overstaying your welcome offends the following acts and disrespects your client's wishes. Feeding your need for spotlight only tests the patience of all involved. Find the value in your brevity and use it to your benefit. The sun will rise tomorrow when you have the chance to take stage once again.

57

Foster Your Taste

This can be acquired through training, much like intellect. Increasing your knowledge increases your hunger and doubles your enjoyment. You will recognize the greatest magicians by their advancement in taste. Only an exceptional performance can satisfy an exceptional performer. The magician with superior taste can offer judgement that makes the loudest magician tremble and cower, or even the most refined lose confidence. Taste can be shared and taught. You would be wise to seek out the company of those rich with flavour. But do not verge into snobbery; the dangers of this attitude will make one tumble towards failure.

58

Ensure That Your Contract is Completed to Your Client's Satisfaction

Some magicians only concern themselves with their act as it was meant to be over the result of audience enjoyment and client expectations. But the final feeling of your crowd and client is the true measure of your services. The world does not recognize the work put in, only the positive or negative results. If your audience and client are fully satisfied, then you lose nothing. In the world of entertainment, if you perform long enough, you encounter situations where you may have to break the rules you live by if you cannot deliver the performance you have promised.

59

Be Meticulous in Your Appearance

Much can be learned by looking at the quality and care of a magician's footwear. Style, sensibility, condition, and sheen will indicate level of professionalism. Like hieroglyphics written from head to toe, we send messages about whom we are and what our true intentions may be to all who lay eyes on us. At all times we should concern ourselves with this matter, for a magician is never just a magician when he takes the stage or holds cards. No, we are magicians at all times and our audience is always around every corner. We cannot take back a first impression made upon a person of value and we never know when we shall come to meet each other. Therefore, be scrupulous with your image at all times and do not overlook the smallest of details. Dirty fingernails will detract from the greatest ambitious card routine.

60

Showmanship Trumps All Tricks

A lackluster performance of the greatest illusion will pale in comparison to the supreme showmanship of a simple card revelation. Understand that Houdini's escapes were built from dramatic means and stole the hearts of all because of this very reason. But when he vanished the elephant, it fell on blind eyes and deaf ears because he placed precedent on method and forgot the why. The art of magic is ninety-five percent psychology, and only five percent trick. Know the truth: the magic of drama will always be more effective and dynamic than the magic of tricks for the effect truly takes place in the mind.

61

Learn How to Say *No*

A great magician does not give his performance to everyone or to every cause. To have practice saying *no* is to prepare for when you need to feel brave. It is just as important as learning how to say *yes*. The most important key to this maxim is that everything will depend on how you deliver your refusal. Some magicians say *no* to everything, and this is a mistake, for it makes you appear deceitful, distrustful, or elementary. Allow for politeness and use choice words to defer from a demanding request.

62

Make Yourself Available and Approachable

The most sought after magicians can be found at the busiest conventions and largest auditoriums. To be inaccessible cuts the cord of emotional connection. Earn approval and favour by being social with the masses. A condition of being master magician is that they should be accessible to all. Welcome your guests before the show, bid farewell after the curtains have closed. One moment to pose for a picture with an adoring, young fan creates a lifelong memory for them but takes less than a minute for us. The wise magician also knows that the majority of his future work comes directly after his performance is finished. Trade your cocktail magic for a reason to court your future clients after your stage act is complete. But always remember that what you say before, during, and after the performance is all part of the show and your character as the magician.

63

Make the Magic About You

The most frequent advice passed down from magician to magician is to "Be yourself." A common error among magicians stems from relying on an insincere script. It is futile to try to act out your individual personality through someone else's character. The world does not need another Criss Angel or Penn & Teller; those characters are already on display for all to see. The populous will not search out an imitation when they can readily enjoy the original. Recognize the opportunity and advantage of making you the hero of the act. Personalize your performance to display your true self to the audience and they will love you forever.

64

Stay Humble

Keep a realistic and reasonable perspective of yourself and your matters. Magicians tend to have high opinions of themselves, especially the ones who have nothing to back it up with. Many dream of their big break and think amazing thoughts of themselves. Their fault lies in hope, which creates inflated promises they never reach. Instead of filling their time by learning, practicing, and rehearsing, they let their mind wonder off into fantastic imaginations, which only bring misery when they meet reality. Yes, hope for the best, but expect the worst. Experience will teach that expectations can run ramped and the magician will frequently suffer from failures. The young magician should exercise caution to protect against utter disaster. Reflect on your true self to fully understand your position and status.

65

Perform With a Good-Natured Attitude

O n stage, this is a virtue, not a vice. Every pinch of cheer is welcome in all performances. Remember too, that even the highest status audience members will join in the fun at times because they feel it makes them liked by all. But if they are placed in a situation that may compromise their dignity, they will turn fast and hard accompanied with penalty. Seasoned magicians will often use a joke to get themselves out of these difficult situations.

66

Make Use of Your Competition

Manage these matters by gripping the handle, not the blade which cuts the hand. The experienced magician knows that one gets more use from their rival magicians than an amateur gets from his friends. Many magicians have reached greatness in part because of their competitors. Praise from friends is typically dangerous as it often comes from biased minds, which can reinforce false assessments. The wise magician understands that harsh criticisms from rivals are better reflections than the kindness of colleagues. Always seeking improvement, the growing magician erases the errors his detractors speak of.

67

Acquire Your Knowledge From Original Sources

The Internet provides a portrait of opinions and typically not much more. It does little good to base a life on information that is misinterpreted or speculation that is unfounded. Sound knowledge will be found in publications that stand the test of time. Trust a reliable source to save resources and headaches. We don't begin climbing a ladder at the middle rung. Dig in deep and take your first step with force to ensure a stable future. The reason Tarbell is synonymous with authority can only be fully realized by the student after diligent studies and application of his knowledge. Trust recent publications that print the voice of our modern professionals.

68

Tailor Your Suit

Appeal first to the eye, then to their mind. It only takes a few seconds for an audience to decide whether or not they like you. Do not place yourself at the bottom of a mountain simply by looking unfit. A few dollars to alter your attire will gain you more goodwill than a few hundred dollars spent on another gimmick. Entertainment is a popularity contest and the fashionable win instant points of status. When you are enjoyable to look at, allowances will be made in the areas where you falter. Never miss an opportunity to compensate for your shortcomings.

69

Culture and Charisma

We are all born equal, but we develop through culture. Therefore, culture is what creates the magician. The greater the magician, the greater he has been cultured. The greatest contribution to our culture is knowledge of the magical arts including things such as skill, method, performance, history and theory. But simply having a wealth of knowledge is not enough for a magician, for they must also have an abundance of charisma. The successful magician carries himself in such a charismatic manner on and off stage at all times. Culture and charisma will be on display as equally in performance as it is in daily conversation. To some entertainers, this charisma comes naturally, internally and externally, in their dialogue, style of dress, and their thoughts. The opposite is a muddy smear that is seen in all they do, typically developed as staunch neatness and strict adherence to social norms.

70

Fully realize yourself

Understand which talents you posses and the strength of each. You cannot master your talents and skills unless you can identify them. We see ourselves each time we look in a mirror, but there are no mirrors for our inner self. Take time each day to inspect your abilities and aptitude. Forget about your outward appearance for a time to focus on personal growth. Analyze your strengths and weakness in your performances on-stage and off stage, both are equally important. And then push forward to test their reach so you can learn their limits.

71

Persistence and Consistency is the Secret of a Long Career in Entertainment

Make wise choices and constantly move forward at a steady pace. Conversely, those that end their careers quickly are either not intelligent enough or don't have the strength to persevere through the hard times. Each good choice will bring a reward, just as every poor choice will set one back. The entertainer who lives fast brings about his end twice as soon.

72

Be Versatile

A magician of many talents equals many entertainers. By sharing his own interests with his ring of magicians, he enhances their lives. Variety in the magical arts keeps the thrill alive. Train your taste and increase your knowledge by opening your mind to all things magic.

73

Build Up and Maintain Your Reputation

Reputation is only borrowed from fame. Reputation comes from notable abilities. Reputation is expensive to obtain, but easily maintained. Reputation holds you to obligations, but also brings recognized status. Reputation should be protected at all costs, for once destroyed it is not easily regained.

74

Appearance Matters Most

To your audience, fans, and clients, you will be judged and held in regard according to what they see, not for how things actually are. Rarely will people care about what happens behind the curtain because often people get attached to how things appear. It does no good being right if headlines still read that your actions were wrong. People are too busy and will not make the effort to understand, so they make all considerations in the short moments between the flicks of their thumb.

75

Perfect What You Have

The need for acquiring trending tricks is a hindrance and a distraction. The average magician already has ten tricks at his disposal that can be made worthy of presenting professionally. Understand that some of the greatest magic ever created and performed came from deep within the magician's heart and mind and needs not the use of contrived gimmicks.

76

One Half of the World's Magicians Laugh at the Other Half and Vice Versa

Do not second guess your work from the voice of a select few, because according to who you ask, you will find that all types of magic are good or all types of magic are bad. For each routine that one magician performs, there will be another standing in the wings criticizing. The magician who believes all magic should fall in line with his taste and preferences is nothing more than a detractor of this art. There are many magicians spread throughout this world and just as many different tastes. For every fellow magician who gives you praise for your performance, there will be another wishing to rip you down. The good magician knows that the only praise he should give credence is from his audience, his client, and expert magicians who specialize in the same field.

77

Learn the Responsibilities of the Many, Different Jobs Within the Entertainment Industry

---

Each cog of the wheel is needed to turn the clock. Understand that different qualities are required for each position. Know which qualities are needed for each job to complete the varied tasks. Some tasks require sensitivity, while others demand boldness. Those that entail correct behaviour are the easiest; those that are most difficult require ingenuity. The easiest can be accomplished with charisma and character, whereas the difficult may require all your dedication and enthusiasm only to fall short of your reach.

78

Do Not Be Boring

The long-winded magician creates many heavy eyelids; leave that job to the hypnotists. Only use as many words as necessary. Being concise and exact gets more accomplished. Great magic, when short, becomes twice as good. The heart of the magic effect is more effective than a barrage of extraneous diversions. The great magician does not bore his audience, especially to distinguished guests who have more important matters to attend to after the performance. If you have important patter to say, say it sooner.

79

Make the Distinction Between Confidence and Arrogance

Confidence is being in control of your body, your tone, your grooming, your manner, and your disposition. Stand up straight with your shoulders back. Arrogance is confidence in excess. The arrogant will fail to connect with their audience. The fine line between confidence and arrogance is an audience that adores you and will hold you in their hearts or loathe you and cast you from their memories.

80

The Shortest Path to Becoming a Great Magician is By Working With Others

Collaborating with the right magicians works particularly well. Together you will grow by sharing tastes, talents, and knowledge. The wise magician knows how to agree with others judiciously and disagree gracefully. Learn through each other's experiences to grow twice as fast.

81

Do Not Be a Hater

There are magicians that are armed and ready with negativity towards everything, not for any particular malicious reason but because this is their natural demeanour. They are trolls to everyone—for things people have said and done, and things people will do. These magicians can turn the greatest of performances into the most unbearable evenings. The great magician, conversely, always finds ways to pardon the unfortunate failing performers with worthy excuses. Lift up your fellow magician, so we can grow and prosper together.

82

Have Another Magician
As a Close Friend

Friends are our second selves. They are good for our soul and filled with knowledge we cannot possess. Gain friendship by doing friendly deeds for your fellow magicians. Entertainers never succeed alone. They depend on peers during the many tough times only other entertainers can understand. We cannot live alone or else our career will die quickly; therefore, we can either live among friends or enemies. Reach out to others everyday in hopes of making a new magician become a friend, colleague, or confidant. Be careful of becoming a charity, for it is infinitely more difficult to lift others up and much more likely they will only drag you down. Find a friend that will be happy for your success.

83

Save For the Slow Down

Work will come in waves. It is both wiser and easier to build your bank account on the high tide. When momentum is strong, you will have many clients, many bookings, many friends, and many favours coming easily. Therefore, build close relationships that do not fade in dark times. The world of entertainment can turn a harsh shoulder at any moment's notice, and it is during these times that the unlucky will not be recognized by former associates.

84

Never Compete With Magicians

Competition only damages your reputation. Your rival will seize every opportunity to stain your name as to appear superior. There is no honour between entertainers. Ever ready they are to shout out the faults of others. If you hear a fellow magician criticize others, be assured they've done the same concerning you. Successful magicians live in harmony with their fellow entertainers because they know there is only competition if you choose to put yourself in competition with another. An original act stands alone and above imitators. It is the copyist who places himself in competition. The copyist is one who begins to belittle and brings life to old scandals. Conversely, magicians that choose goodwill are regarded to have dignity and good reputation.

85

Do Not Talk About Yourself in the Company of Magicians

You will either praise yourself, which is simply bragging, or blame yourself which lowers your status in the social hierarchy. The clever magician can make jokes of self-depreciation in times of repartee, but the wise magician never initiates the casual conversation focused on his own failures or accomplishments. The fastest way to lose friends is to speak continually of your latest standing ovation.

86

Never Become Disliked

This is the death of an entertainer. There is no good reason a magician should try to become disliked by the masses. It can happen easily enough on its own. The common fault of the over-confident and inexperienced magician often lies in the need to be egocentric onstage and narcissistic offstage. This attitude only creates harm to others and gains them little advantages in life. Remember to be admired and respected, you must admire and respect others.

87

Stay With the Times

Successful magicians understand the importance of keeping up with modern styles and affairs. Magicians are infamous for being trapped in a world and time of their own, one that is out of sync with the current day. This invites ridicule and develops a poor reputation. Everything changes, as time marches forward; therefore, be sure to stay in step. The heartbeat of entertainment pulses with modern tastes and trends. It is the popular vote that wins the day. The successful magician that stands on his own, by doing his own thing, is only successful because his magic is created with the intention of being a trendsetter and leader to new styles. Even though the field of magic is rich with acts of the past, challenge yourself to look forward and advance the art to new heights.

88

Be Distinct With Patter and Routines

This is the surest way to stand out and win good favour from clients and peers alike. Create your own uniqueness in all that you do: in speech, in fashion, in promotion, in presentation, and even in your walk. Master magicians know the way to win the audience's heart is by opening their own. Exude your confidence on stage and be the truest magician you can be, born from hard work and superior worth. Audiences have a natural talent to recognize artificial character that is designed only to impress. When the spectator feels they are watching a fake, they will feel cheated of their money and time.

89

Charisma and Refinement
in All You Do

This is the quintessential quality of the master magician. It is the blood of talent, the air of speech, the spirit of manipulations, and the life of all performances. This is hard to learn, as it is mostly a gift from birth, but is so important that it matters more than skill and knowledge. It is greater than the cleverest method of trickery or master crafted routine. Charisma and refinement create a shortcut to accomplishments and acts as an immediate rescue from embarrassments.

90

Go Out and Perform

To be able to perform magic skills and techniques, and to know how to show them makes a magician twice as good. But a person who can perform magic and doesn't perform for an audience is not a true magician. Only telling others that you can manipulate a deck of cards is the same as if you cannot. Come up from your basement, come away from the computer, and interact with the world in real time to create real magic.

91

Be Seen; Be Heard

If the audience cannot see what is happening, then it does not exist to them. If the spectators do not hear, then they will not comprehend. Come out of the shadows and step into the spotlight for all to see, and speak loud and clear for all to hear. One without the other is an incomplete story and only leaves the crowd feeling confused. Do not neglect the logistics of presenting your material to crowds of all sizes or you will limit your reach and stunt your career. If faced with adversity, know the truth that with magic it is more important to be heard than be seen.

92

Learn How to Walk on Stage

Your posture and gait are a direct reflection of your care and consideration. The professional ensures that all aspects of presentation are mastered, and movement across a stage is of no exception. Step into the spotlight with your best foot forward, shoulders back, chest out, head held high. The way you carry yourself on stage will help carry your performance. And remember: do not turn your back on the audience, or they may turn on you.

93

Bring Backups

Only the foolish magician would bring a single resource that could easily be doubled. The wise magician brings a backup to serve as an emergency replacement. You should not depend on one prop or material, however important it may be. Each act should have a planned backup because disaster is sure to strike when least expected. If we depend on these resources for our success, we should treat them with equal care and attention.

94

Every Magician Will Have Bad Shows

It may be true that there is no such thing as a bad audience, but it is true that bad luck days will strike an entertainer; they do exist. Even if the magician tries changing his act for the better, nothing will help. Chance has something to say for every performance, no matter how prepared and polished a magician is. The most masterful magicians have experienced sour hours and so will you. It is also important to recognize when luck is on your side. Seize every opportunity and do not throw away the lucky chances you are sure to win. But don't judge your day on a single piece of luck, good or bad, because it might only be a single slice that makes no difference to the rest of your day.

95

Never Repeat the Same Trick for the Same Audience

The levitation of a person is the same as the levitation of an object from their point of view. How ridiculous it would be to watch an evening of objects float for a full hour. Only slightly less absurd would be to repeat a levitation act in different dress within the same performance. To a spectator, all cards tricks are the same, but this does not mean one cannot provide an evening of entertainment with only a deck of cards. It is our job to create the distinction between each effect. Avoid the mundane and add depth to your magic performance through variety.

96

Free Shows Will Get You Free Shows

Recognize that there is a time and place in your career to be putting in hours on the stage no matter the cost. In the beginning, experience is its own reward. But do not place value solely in the currency of exposure, for all you will gain is a reputation for performing such shows. Understand your value as an entertainer and know yourself to the greatest depths. To earn a professional wage you must first become a professional. How will you know when you are finally a professional magician? You won't. What makes a magician a professional? Attitude and work ethic. Recognize the high value you must place on practicing and performing as much as you can, everyday if possible.

97

Your Work Happens Off Stage and Your Reward is Taking the Stage

The experienced magician knows that performance only takes ten percent of his time but accounts for ninety percent of his work. The experienced client knows this and is willing to compensate as such. The inexperienced client only sees the reverse; do not be offended when you are offered similar compensation. Preparation may be the key to success, but only accomplished with proper balance. Cast your net wide with the duties of a growing magician and know there will always be ten times the amount of work needed to be done than what you initially considered.

98

Quality, Service, and Volume;
Pick Two for Success

Successful magicians can provide two very well. Most magicians only provide one. No one can do all three efficiently and effectively. Master magicians recognize the value in providing their clients the highest quality and the best service; thereby, do not have to concern themselves with performing a high volume of shows. The beginner recognizes the value in performing a high volume of shows while he develops a higher quality show and learns what it takes to provide the necessary service to valued clients. The fool believes they can provide a superior level of all three for their clients and thus sets themselves up for failure.

99

Learn the Art of Conversation

That is where your clients and fans find the true you. Aside from your act, there is nothing else in the business of entertainment that requires the most attention despite being a common aspect of life. If it takes such great care and practice to write scripts and patter for your show, which is a planned conversation, then just imagine how important it is to have your conversation skills on display during all occasions. Your clients will know exactly who you are just by the way you converse in a casual setting. If you want to be a true professional, learn to speak like one in daily conversations and in all occasions. If you wish to have upper class clients, learn to speak in their manner. Adapt your vocabulary and tone for those you are speaking with. Likewise, don't be critic towards your fellow magicians or strictly a collector of ideas, or else people will avoid you.

In conversation, taking care of what you say is more important than how you say it.

100

Learn the Classics

The concepts, ideas, and skills that have been published in these quality works, which we deem classics of magic, deal with psychological universals, such as how we fool audiences, how we create magical experiences, how to structure routines, etc. Essentially all the elements required for a strong magic performance. These lessons are unchanging and vitally important in the development of a successful magician. The studied and cultured magician will always be ten steps ahead of the magician who only learns from lectures and free online videos. The classics are not just a look into the past, but also the doorway into the greatest performances and acts ever created by magicians. Therefore, the classic books in magic are for anyone who wants to understand what it truly means to be a magician.

101

Know Your Worth

Your value is not dependent upon what other magicians charge for their shows in your local area. If you don't charge for your time, then that is exactly what it is worth. The price tag of a performer is a direct representation of the value and the quality of entertainment the client receives, which is directly related to the success of their event. You can earn what you're truly worth as long as you understand what your value is, you are able to provide that value, and your clients agree to that value. If you can't appreciate yourself with a higher price tag, then your clients won't either.

102

Be More Careful Not to Give a Bad Performance Than to Give One Hundred Great Performances

---

No one talks long about a good magic performance, but everyone will easily recall that one horrible performance. The general audience expects a clean magic show and will not converse about which routines went right, but will quickly talk about what went wrong. Mistakes carry farther than any applause. Likewise, a magician can give the greatest performances the world has seen, but if his reputation is stained with accusations, he will be known first by the error of his ways. The wise entertainer chooses his words carefully and restricts his feelings from print. Many careers have been destroyed by a misinterpreted comment or incriminating photograph. Keep both hands where everyone can see them.

103

Always Be Open to Learning

There is no magician who cannot teach another something, and there is no magician so excellent that he cannot learn and grow further. To know how to make use of other magicians is useful. Brilliant entertainers can see positives in other acts and they know how difficult it is to make anything good. Arrogant magicians will cast others aside, not noticing the good and only pointing out the bad. It is a good habit to converse with others presuming they know something that you do not.

104

Know the Value in Performing Abroad

Your hometown will always be the humbling stage; it remembers your small beginnings rather than the greatness you may have reached. Performing only in your hometown is the fertilizer of your envy. A glass of wine may be regarded as having more value if it comes from afar. Foreign entertainers are held in higher regard and earn more respect, partly because they come from far away, partly because they are already perfected. The wooden carving on the mantle gets higher recognition from those who have not known or seen it as the tree in the backyard.

105

Perform Difficult Tasks as if They Were Easy and Easy Tasks as if They Were difficult

A truly talented magician understands that this secret opens a new world of acts to perform. At first, we always seek to perform the most difficult or the most impossible, yet years of experience teaches us that it matters not so much what we do, but rather how we do it. It is easier to escape from a straight jacket hanging upside down, but the entertainer knows this appears more difficult to the lay-person. A repeated production and vanish of a stack of cards, by the means of split fans, is a difficult technique that only looks beautiful if performed with ease. It matters not of how things are, only how they appear.

106

Never Defend Yourself in Print

This defense will only glorify the attacker and does little to stop him. Your words leave a messy trail that is not so easily erased. Many critics will play the game as a cynic, stating harsh reviews to gain notoriety. The art of surviving troll attacks is to take no notice of it. Fighting them will only make things worse.

107

Keep Your Finest Magic Secrets
to Yourself

This is a maxim of the greatest magicians that ever lived. Every magic teacher also understands this: how to remain superior and remain the master of the art. The wise magician retains his status, maintains the respect of his peers, and keeps his clients close. To keep a reserve of magic skill and knowledge is a key to success, especially when the pool is full of other entertainers.

108

Never Let Your Magic Be Seen Until it is Mastered

The audience can only enjoy magic when it is complete. Our initial attempts at scripting, routining, and manipulating are not of perfect form and do a disservice to our true capabilities if performed prematurely. When people finally get a chance to see the finished act, they will still have the stained image of how they saw it when it was in the works. Before your magic trick is created, it is nothing, and while you are working on it, it is still nothing. To rush out and perform prematurely is to gamble with revealing the secret to the effect. Once the secret to the method is revealed, the magical moment can never be created. All is lost.

109

Learn the Business of Show Business

A successful magician should not focus solely on magic; there should be knowledge of the business side as well. Well studied magicians are missing out on the opportunities for many performances, for while they may know dozens of ways to perform a colour change, they do not know how to sell or market their act, which is a real necessity. The constant study of skills, techniques, and routines leaves them no time to take care of business matters. If the greatest good of magic happens in performing for others, then let the magician understand how to sell his show so he can perform often and regularly. Develop proper habits and learn the secrets of business success so you can bring your magic to the masses. What good is magic that is practiced and rehearsed if it is not performed?

110

Finish What You Start

Some magicians put all their effort into researching and purchasing a new effect, but never find the time or energy to implement it in their show. They invent new material, but never complete the process to bring it to stage. Everything they do ends the first time they stop. The dedication to see things through to the end is difficult. The patience needed is much. The young magician puts the hard work in to acquire, learn, and practice, but then they feel content and lack the ambition to bring it in front of an audience. They prove that they can be a magician, but choose not to be. This shows that either they can't perform magic or are insecure. If the magic is good, then why not perform it? If it's not good magic, then why learn it at all?

111

Have No Empty Days

Each day is a gift to explore the world of magic and work towards your preeminent showing. Our skill, talent, knowledge, charisma, fitness, and even beauty must be ready for the stage on any given day. The unprepared magician sets himself up for failure by not monopolizing on his precious time. Carelessness and failing to stay in top shape leads us to our own destruction. The masterful magician knows to be ready at a moment's notice because that is when opportunity can be greatest.

112

The Successful Magician Does it Now; the Foolish Magician Does it Later

---

Both do the same thing, the only difference lies in when they do it. Be able to make a quick decision and then make sure it was the right decision. The one who cannot make a decision will starve himself by being indecisive. The smart magician recognizes what needs to be done now, which he does willingly and gains a good reputation from it.

113

Keep Your Act Fresh

As we grow, our taste will change, and so should our magic to fit our taste. Let it change for the better. Some are in constant change; others stay with their first love, but most are wise to make change every seven years. Quite often your new magic act will not be recognized for its greatness until it reaches the height of its maturity. The wise magician makes use of this newly created performance because people place a higher value in things that are new. The fresh magic is uncommon and the new flavour is welcomed. It is a truth that brand new mediocrity gains more positive attention than accustomed excellence. But keep in mind that the novelty of being new will be short lived. Therefore, take advantage of every opportunity when debuting a new you. Collect your applause, record your testimonials, fill your calendar for the season and know that this season will soon pass.

114

Beware of Overexposure

People will grow tired of familiar magic performances; therefore, it is wise to regulate your exposure. Make use of being unavailable to increase your value and admiration. Talents lose their lustre from over-use because it is easier for audiences to notice the weathered exterior than the great talent inside. Travel abroad to leave the local audience to their imaginations and stories of the great performances you once gave them. Turn your absence into desire by regulating your appearances appropriately.

115

Nothing Depreciates a Magician More Than Being Seen as a Common Layperson

Entertainers are a special breed and must be regarded as such. The day we are seen to be like a nine-to-five, office worker is the day we blend in with the masses. The successful magician must stand apart from the crowd. The successful magician must hold an uncommon reputation for not meeting the norms of society, for with ingenuity comes intrigue and a new level of respect. Do not be a next-door neighbour with hobby; be the man of mystery everyone expects a true magician to be.

116

Work on Your Act

Your act comes first, everything else follows. Without a compelling performance, tickets will not sell, attention will not be gained, your name will soon be forgotten, your phone will not ring, and your email will be empty. Without an act, it is pointless to work on marketing. For even with the shows you sell, when you fail to deliver a promised spectacle, your unprepared act will hurt you tenfold. A truly spectacular act will gain you opportunity for more performances, but a sub-par performance can create irreparable damage.

Maxims of a Magician

1. Intelligence and charisma.

2. Make your own choices.

3. Conceal your projects in the works.

4. Wisdom and bravery.

5. Have others depend on you.

6. A magician continually grows.

7. Do not upstage your headliner.

8. Self-control is freedom to perform.

9. Avoid the faults of the magic community.

10. Fortune and fame.

11. Build relationships with magicians who can teach you.

12. Magic and materials.

13. Attention to circumstance.

14. Be accessible to magical thinkers.

15. Mean well and stay keen.

16. Apply yourself and be skillful.

17. Be modest with your beginnings.

18. Be a magician of modern times.

19. Learn to be lucky.

20. Learn to live with misery.

21. Control your imagination.

22. Know how to read into conversations.

23. Excellence lives in quality.

24. Refuse to be common.

25. Avoid the unlucky.

26. Develop a reputation for helping out other magicians.

27. Know how to pull away.

28. Know your greatest quality.

29. Think over your act.

30. Keep a file of prepared lines and know when to use them.

31. Recognize when a routine is at its peak and know when to use it.

32. Never finish with your strongest effect.

33. Give permission for applause.

34. Always warm up your audience.

35. Finish your performance while the crowd is still on your side.

36. Natural on-stage presence.

37. Control your hostilities towards other magicians.

38. Become a magician with great depth.

39. Do not lose your self-respect and don't become too self-conscious.

40. Choose your material well.

41. Ensure your routines mean something to you.

42. If you are not funny, don't try to be.

43. Master your openings.

44. Never be upset or make a scene in the public eye.

45. Respect your audience's intelligence.

46. Always thank the sponsors.

47. Be persistent and intelligent.

48. Learn to slow down.

49. Appear professional at all times.

50. Adapt yourself to your crowd.

51. Prepare a brilliant finale.

52. Shine bright in what is excellent.

53. Leave the enjoyment for your audience.

54. Keep a collection of 'outs' at your disposal.

55. Do not perform filler.

56. Respect your restraints.

57. Foster your taste.

58. Ensure that your contract is completed to your client's satisfaction.

59. Be meticulous in your appearance.

60. Showmanship trumps all tricks.

61. Learn how to say *no*.

62. Make yourself available and approachable.

63. Make the magic about you.

64. Stay humble.

65. Perform with a good-natured attitude.

66. Make use of your competition.

67. Acquire your knowledge from original sources.

68. Tailor your suit.

69. Culture and charisma.

70. Fully realize yourself.

71. Persistence and consistency is the secret of a long career in entertainment.

72. Be versatile.

73. Build up and maintain your reputation.

74. Appearance matters most.

75. Perfect what you have.

76. One half of the world's magicians laugh at the other half and vice versa.

77. Learn the responsibilities of the many, different jobs within the entertainment industry.

78. Do not be boring.

79. Make the distinction between confidence and arrogance.

80. The shortest path to becoming a great magician is by working with others.

81. Do not be a hater.

82. Have another magician as a close friend.

83. Save for the slow down.

84. Never compete with magicians.

85. Do not talk about yourself in the company of magicians.

86. Never become disliked.

87. Stay with the times.

88. Be distinct with patter and routines.

89. Charisma and refinement in all you do.

90. Go out and perform.

91. Be seen; be heard.

92. Learn how to walk on stage.

93. Bring backups.

94. Every magician will have bad shows.

95. Never repeat the same trick for the same audience.

96. Free shows will get you free shows.

97. Your work happens off stage and your reward is taking the stage.

98. Quality, service, and volume; pick two for success.

99. Learn the art of conversation.

100. Learn the classics.

101. Know your worth.

102. Be more careful not to give a bad performance than to give one hundred great performances.

103. Always be open to learning.

104. Know the value in performing abroad.

105. Perform difficult tasks as if they were easy and easy tasks as if they were difficult.

106. Never defend yourself in print.

107. Keep your finest magic secrets to yourself.

108. Never let your magic be seen until it is mastered.

109. Learn the business of show business.

110. Finish what you start.

111. Have no empty days.

112. The successful magician does it now; the foolish magician does it later.

113. Keep your act fresh.

114. Beware of overexposure.

115. Nothing depreciates a magician more than being seen as a common layperson.

116. Work on your act.

Recommended Magic Books

(The Classics and More)

1. The Complete Jinx by Ted Annemann

2. New Modern Coin Magic by J.B. Bobo

3. Mastering the Art of Magic by Eugene Burger

4. Magic and Meaning Eugene Burger

5. Absolute Magic by Derren Brown

6. Carneycopia by John Carney

7. Book of Secrets by John Carney

8. The Workers Series by Michael Close

9. 13 Steps to Mentalism by Corinda

10. The Complete Works of Derek Dingle

11. The Expert at the Card Table by S. W. Erdnase

12. The Trick Brain by Dariel Fitzkee

13. Showmanship for Magicians by Dariel Fitzkee

14. Magic by Misdirection by Dariel Fitzkee

15. Casino Game Protection by Steve Forte

16. The Ramsay Legend by Andrew Galloway

17. The Dai Vernon Book of Magic by Lewis Ganson

54. The Tarbell Course in Magic Volumes 1-7 by Harlan Tarbell

55. Revelation by Dai Vernon

56. Maximum Entertainment by Ken Weber

In the beginnings the young magician is but a caterpillar, at twenty a beautiful butterfly, at thirty a tiger, at forty an eagle, at fifty a fox, at sixty an elephant, at seventy an owl, at eighty a tortoise.

The End

About The Author

Richy Roy (The Wealthy Magician) supports his writing hobby by working as a full-time entertainer, specializing in magic, balloon twisting, DJing, and hosting game shows across Canada.

Besides being a baseball and football fan, Richy loves making online comedy videos, listening to music (especially hip-hop/rap), and cooking delicious meals for his family.

Richy lives with his wife and three young kids in Weyburn, Saskatchewan.

If you enjoyed this book, you might also enjoy...

THE
WEALTHY MAGICIAN
Manifesto for Professionals
By Richy Roy

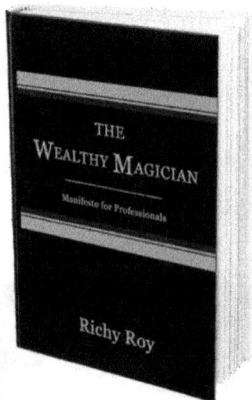

Vanish Magic Magazine says:

"I have read A LOT of books about business and magic over the past 25 years and a lot of the earlier ones are outdated. Now and then one will come along that will really inspire and show you exactly how to make a living from this business. This book does EXACTLY that...This book really does cover everything. Without a doubt one of the best books filled with advice from somebody who walks the walk."

www.ingramcontent.com/pod-product-compliance
Lightning Source LLC
Chambersburg PA
CBHW060936040426
42445CB00011B/891